AF433618

WORDS OF LIFE

Markell L. Mooney

Inner child press, ltd.

3

General Information

Words of Life
Markell L. Mooney
2nd Edition : 2023

This Publishing is protected under Copyright Law as a "Collection". All rights for all submissions are retained by the Individual Author and or Artist. No part of this Publishing may be Reproduced, Transferred in any manner without the prior **WRITTEN CONSENT** of the "Material Owner" or its Representative Barnes & Noble Press. Any such violation infringes upon the Creative and Intellectual Property of the Owner pursuant to International and Federal Copyright Law. Any queries pertaining to this "Collection" should be addressed to the Publisher of Record.

**Publisher Information
2nd Edition:**

This Collection is protected under U.S. and International Copyright Laws
Copyright © 2018 : Markell L. Mooney
ISBN # 9798823160858 Barnes & Noble Press
$ 14.99

5

Dedication

This book is dedicated to the blessed memory of my beloved father Willie E. Mooney Sr. Thank you for raising me and showing me the true qualities of being the man I am today. I love you and will miss you dearly!

To my Godmother Rosetta Gadlen. Thank you for being the greatest Godmother that anyone could ever have. You are definitely in heaven showing them how it's done.

To My Children Jaikel and Indy Crawford
You both mean the world to me. You are my heart and my soul. I'm truly proud to be your father and hope what I instilled in you both should you decide to have children one day, I am confident that you will do the same. I Love you both so very much.

Table of Contents

Table of Contents . . . *continued*

WORDS OF LIFE – PART 3

Epilogue

Acknowledgements

First and foremost, I must give glory to my Lord and Savior Jesus Christ who makes all things possible.

To the queen who gave me life, Ms. Martha L. Mooney. Thank you so much for raising me with not only your nourishment from birth but from the nourishment, you instilled in me throughout my teenage years into adulthood. You continue to keep a stronghold on me even after letting me jump the nest in an attempt to fly from the tree of life to spread my wings towards the world. Again, thank you mama, and I love you.

My God-brothers, Robert Gadlen Jr. and Anthony McPhee.
To Valencia Lockhart, thank you for being there through tough and joyful times.
Steve Wallace, Shaun Hill, Paula Cherry and Bryan Williams.

To Richard Grausman, Chef Sarah Stegner, and Chef George Bumbaris, thanks for giving me the opportunity to excel at the beginning of my career in Hospitality and Culinary Arts. R.I.P to my Home economics teacher Ms. Audria Simpson-Huntington, thank you for opening the doors for me in furthering my education. To the entire Chicago poetry community, we are all family! To my original Patio Poets Sa'alek, King Solomon, Darkchild, Tenette and BlackPeace, thanks for all of your love and support throughout the years of operating the Patio show. Special Acknowledgements to Phoenix, you are the best graphic designer on the planet. May you Rest in Heaven my friend, you are free to fly.

To Marielle Dickens, I am honored to be your mentor, keep pushing forward for success and always keep God first in your life.

To all my Prince Hall Brothers and Sistars of the 3-5-7, let's continue to travel to the east.

To poets of Earcandy Inc., Black Diamond, K-Luv, Creative Scott, Phenom, Awthentik, Allen J. Bryson, Blaq Ice & P.O.E.T., 3BM Family, Spoken & The Cypher Coalition, Danny Devine, Obi-SoulStar, Solace Souls, Team At Ease Poetry.

The queen of Chicago poetry Mama Brenda Matthews R.I.P, it was an honor sharing the stage with such royalty. Avery R. Young, Orron, M'reld Green, Blaq Ice, Dr. Groove, Phoenix, Jun Jun, Lathrese Williams, James "Doe-boy" King and the entire State Of Grind Family, Nova McKinney, Toly Walker .

There are so many others, if I missed you, I'll get you in Volume II.
Peace, blessings and Word Life,

Markell L. Mooney
AKA- Kell-O-G

The
WORDS
PART 1

13

Blackout

Dimming, Dimming, Dimming

The sun flourishes from the sky
And the moon catapults from the ocean

I see no more faces, places, colors, and images
At least the ones that are blind through my mind
Through my third eye combined
They create roller coaster rides
Through inter-galactic galaxies
While eyes rest

In the midst of darkness
I celebrate life, love, and pain

My dreams are taking flight

Dedications
A Haiku for the Soul

Shackled, outlasted
Emmett Till and Rosa sparked
King, X, ignition

Fatigue

Like a shadow waiting for movement
From its master
The triple overtime blues
And I'm in the starting five
Playing over 40 minutes
Constantly running
Constantly struggling
Trying to make ends meet

Driving through back roads with dead ends
Not studying for an exam having to cheat
Microwavable habits instead of home-cooked eats

A never-ending journey of laziness
That's a stereotypical feat
But I smoke through the peace pipe of reality
And I drink the wine of refreshment

I know the world is mine

Family

There are many things we cherish
Material possessions, fame, and money
Our significant other, cars and clothes

When there's nothing to materialize
Nothing to drive
Nothing to spend
In the end
Your family is there for you

When bridges are not burned
And you find yourself in a hole
Your family can dig you out

When finances are low
Family is there to give you a boost
Family should not be taken advantage of
Show that you are appreciative by giving back

Nothing is better than family

Shadow

Dedicated to little brothers that have lost their big brother

Like a shadow
I mimic him
His style, his grace
His serious face
Just as the moon copies the sun
I followed the footsteps of big brother

Where he walked, I walked
What he talked, I talked
His eyes were mine, even when I was blind
And could not understand much
When I was younger

When the streetlights came on at night
Curiosity took flight in my mind
Wondering what big brother was doing
Pass one in the morning

As the years passed, my shadow faded away from me
I didn't see you as much
But when I did you didn't want me to
Follow behind and mimic you

The sun shifts from east to west
 And my shadow takes a final rotation
 Because of worldly implications

A bullet took big brother's life
Now little brother's shadow remains faded
With no one to mimic

LITE

I eat lite, sleep lite, breathe lite, drink lite
Walk lite, talk lite, live lite, and love lite

My friends lite, my family's lite
My circle's lite, surrounding me tight

My music's lite
Neo-soul, old school hip-hop
"Don't push me cause I'm close to the edge"
 LITE!!

Jazz lite, Coltrane, Langston Hughes, King Oliver
Ma Rainey, Donald Bird, Bessie Smith

Soul R & B lite
Teddy Pendergrass, no Trey Songz,
Luther Vandross, Chaka Khan
LITE!!

90's Trios and Quad Groups Lite
Jodeci, Boyz II Men and Shai
LITE!

I mold lite; I mentor lite
I teach lite; I preach lite
The youth approach me to say thank you,
Mr. Mooney, for helping me graduate and cross the stage

21
I must be doing something right?

Work lite, play lite
Read lite, write lite
My paper lite, my pens lite
I'm a DJ so I spit, and I spin Lite!!

Conscious lite
I eat healthy but it's a must to have
Soul food Sunday's Lite!!

I Love lite
My soulmate is lite
I know she's my future wife
Single parent, two kids and doing a great job
Lite!!

Spiritual lite, God Fearing lite
This world is not promised for anyone
We must prepare for the lite

As I'm writing this poem
In the darkness of all things

I think of a Song by the great
Curtis Mayfield, which says
"Right on for the darkness."
What he's really saying is

Right on towards the Lite

Tears

Eyes shed tears not shown
Emotions lost like kites flying in the wind
Many chances given for love once again
Tears shed raindrops forming oceans that rise
Never to dry in the sunlit sky

23

WORDS
of
LOVE
PART 2

Can you find me?

Can you find me in the air you breathe?
Can you find me when you're in need?

Can you find me when you're feeling down?
To go that extra mile
To pick you up and make you smile?
And make the end results worthwhile?

Can you find me?

To relieve your stress time
When it's PMS time
Lay my head on your breast time

Can you find me?

Not locked up
Not on the block up and down
Not messing around, so you don't go out and get knocked up

Can you find me?

Grounded before and after hours
No need for an elite task force navy seal soul
Searching for me because it's BEN ONE
Toni Braxton was right
Love should bring me home to you every night

I'm making it a mission that you don't have to go looking for me

Can you find me?
Watching our favorite reality TV show
Picking up heavy shopping bags and opening up doors
Washing your clothes, dishes and mopping your floors
That quick see you later kiss I'm on the go

Can you find me?

When it's dinnertime
Family time
When you are going to work, and I ask you to call off so
We can enjoy our spontaneous time
Find me and love me for a lifetime
And after all this time you're searching for me
Your journey ends

Because I found you

Her Smile

Her smile touches the universe
A glow that separates the moon from the sun
From forming an eclipse
It shines the earth
And makes the sun jealous

Your smile is a sin
It strengthens the weak against evil
Like a butterfly that nurtures a flower
You feed the spirit with love
An endless chain of happiness

Your smile is cradled by peace
Like a newborn baby being breastfed
You breed the world with your touch of Love

Ice Cream Dream

I'm looking for that special flavor
That Ice Cream Dream

I want to indulge in a taste like I never tasted before
This flavor will send signals to my tongue senses creating
Serene images to my brain

I can picture chocolate waterfalls in an exotic paradise
I can lick a sugar filled with vanilla ice cream with
Toppings of fudge, caramel, and butterscotch as the flavors flow
through the little tiny specs in my tongue

The sweet, sour and bitter sections all combine as one
The taste is overpowering
Energy builds as I blend chilly serge through my body as I
Descend into a deep sleep of this ice cream dream

As I venture fruit flavors trigger my brain
Peaches and apricot shapes form into the clouds
I can create a sculpture of our body from the heavens
There is no need for 31 selections

I can narrow down this taste without any rejections

Whether it's homemade, sorbet or fat-free
To savor this favorable dream would be so enticing
Knowing that the tang on my tongue
Will choose the one

The one that will trigger an explosion of taste buds
Blasting out of the barrel of a shotgun into my soul
This flavor is so bold I can grasp this dream
Of flavor sensations broadening my imaginations
My dream comes to a closure

I've found that flavor, that taste, this is the one
Give me a scoop

31

Needy Love

For the Love Conscious

I need you like need air to air to breathe
It torments my soul to admit that you do exist
I survive off you like a rose growing in the ghetto
Rather than a field of meadows
I understand my sacrifice for you

Like a caterpillar needing its cocoon for transformation
Converting my heart through reformations
My ultimate goal is not only to understand you
But to be one with you

Dried Up Prunes & Juicy Grapes

She's the juiciest selection that is picked off
From the vine of divinity
One who anticipates affinity
She's nurtured strong and blessed with purity

To find this lonely fruit through
Rules of uncertainty
Like a needle in a haystack
Strictly breastfed no Similac
And it's a justified fact that she is a woman

She is a grape
Not a prune

This prune has no age defined and she is summoned to
Wreak havoc upon the fully preserved lives if ideal men
She's a prune that is dry

Dry as the Sahara Desert
Dry as the tongue licking stamps to letters
Drier than MC Hammer losing his cheddar
She rolls her eyes when you stare
Wearing skin tight dresses and fake hair

Everywhere she goes she's flaunting
No play to blood thirsty vampires they're haunting

Brother's that come with whack lines, tight game

The gift of gab or just being honest,
direct and sincere No home-runs brother's,
just keep bunting

Egoism swells up this woman's head like helium
Balloons at a Bar Mitzvah
There is nothing kosher about this woman's lifestyle

She's misleading modest heart of men who might
Manifest this maiden into marital bliss
So just dismiss the wish for a chance to rock this woman's world
because she will not release and unfurl her mind and humble her
stereotypical thoughts that This prune has potential and more worth
than just a Heart snatcher when we should snatch that juicy fruit
Something ripe, real and ready to consume

Honest, loyal and loving
If you seek a dry prune
Prepare to get flushed out

I Seek You

A Personal Confession

Through the cracks of the urban *Ghettos*
Queen, I seek you

Not that you are not hard to find, but you hide in a disguise of mystery
Where brothers must mend broken maidens and master your mind
because in these modern times
Your independent status outshines the blinds
Who can see the real you

I seek you sister so we can
Savor this sweet state of serenity and swim into a
Seductive space into my soul

I seek you so we can
Cease all sadness that has stopped you from sailing
Through a stream of sanity
In your heart is the one that I hold

I misconstrue the perception that reflects the depths that's crept
through your heart that has been
Haunting you since the beginning of your existence
When ignorance has depicted you as non-equal

I seek you because you are the backbone
Of the household
When we are off track, you are the one that is there
To love, console and keep us in control

I seek you because you mold us
I seek you because you hold us
You unfold our timid souls for us

With you, there is no ending
You are the threshold
And you cure us like a common cold
I seek you because you have a heart of gold
And you put a stronghold even when we are
At the bottom of the totem pole

I seek you because you have the key that sticks into the
Keyhole of divinity
As I wait on the other side of the door
Affinity

To find you

I plead the 5th; I'm Guilty of Love

I have the right to remain silent
Anything I say will be used against me in a court of law
I have the right to an attorney
I have the right to strengthen or end this journey

If I can't afford this love, then someone will be appointed to step up to
the plate and replace me
At no charge

I understand I can choose to commit or be carefree
I understand that I'm in control of my own destiny
I'm guilty and I plead the 5th
I'm guilty of love

I'm guilty of not only understanding you
But not understanding myself
I'm my worst enemy when it comes to seeing the truth when you show
the other side of the story Instead of taking the criticism,
I'm walking away

I'm guilty of the fact that when you stand in front of me, I draw away
from you
When it's my fault, I blame everything
On you and not myself

I focus on me and not us
I don't take heed of our needs
All I see are colorblind images of love

My pride is like a game of chess because the queen is
About to check my ass and if I don't make a move or
Strategic plan to make things right
I will continue to plead guilty

The Aisle

That long walk
That endless walk it seems
Days, weeks and months of preparations precision
Practicing for the ultimate spiritual climaxing moment
Of saying I do

That endless walk down the aisle of love
Two souls transform to flames of affinity
As two lit candles merge as one

Each drop of wax that falls to Gods earth
Equals to every step the bride takes
Down the aisle of love

Each blink on the groom eyes as he sheds tears and
Watches her initial approach
Past and present images you both reminisce on what
Brought you to this day

To that first phone call
To that first kiss
From dusk to nightfall Eyes gel together like glue

Mind, body and soul bind this union
Through the hourglass of time
Creating that endless walk down the aisle of love

Each step closer for the bride as she approaches
Eyes blink, and tears shed by the groom
Virtuous traits of marital bliss

Create that long journey down the aisle
To an end

Just to begin
With the joining of hands in preparation of the title of
Being called soul mates
Kiss and say I do

As they together walk down the aisle of love

Mr. Fantasy

Have you ever just wanted someone to love?
But never have to worry about the responsibility?
No heartbreaks, no pain, no worries
Someone who can tap that and leave?

Then Mr. Fantasy is what you would need
See Mr. Fantasy is just that type of guy
That would never give you the title as
His man, his soul mate, or is boo

If you want a quick fix, without the trouble of
Him knocking down doors asking for more
Mr. Fantasy is the one to call on

The ultimate backup plan if you just want to kick it
A man who does not care about you but only
Getting up in your pants
Only sex, never romance
It's a chance it might be Mr. Fantasy

For social media browsing ladies
Who needs a quickie away from your man?
A truly defined dip with a plan

Don't get attached when he whips it on you

41
Because he'll never commit
And please don't be upset if he has another

Appointment because he's knocking boots
With another lady who just might get hooked also
Remember the name when you Google search because
Mr. Fantasy will give you just what you desire

A Fantasy

Studio Love

I want to create the perfect mix- tape

It doesn't need radio play, billboard charts
Platinum status and concert shows that come with it

If I can calculate the beats per minute
I would have an unlimited lifetime supply of tracks to
Spin within each genre that generate thoughts for you

My DJ board will be our platform
My hands are the ones and twos
And your spine is the mixer
And as my fingers slide the crossfade back and forth
Creating a perfect blend as I glide my hands across the
Contours of your caramelized skin

Beat matching would be flawless
Adjusting each and every track's recording level
So that it sounds just right
Our lows, mid, and highs just right
Master level with each transition just tight

Each genre is an extension of four-play perfection

Of everlasting euphoria of ecstasy

So please, let me handle your pro-tools

Let me *fruit your loops* over and over and over

Like MJ let me rock with you all night long

If the needle drops on old-school hip-hop and
R & B we are doing the two-step
And if the needle drops house music, we jackin'
Reggae action for some satisfaction

Various needs while switching up speeds
We switch positions, and you can handle the boards
And throw on a slow jam
But please don't scratch up my needle
Close out the mood with a Motown review
There is no reason to press play without some
Smokey Robinson and Marvin Gaye

We mix down, finalize and click save
As the needle is raised off the wax
My head drops on your breast
The test begins once we burn this compilation of affinitive ballads

Our thoughts combine for a track title
"Intimate essential Volume one."
And there will be more than just a blank cd of memory
Going inside of your hard drive
It's our collective juices of genres that combine
Us as soul mates

This will definitely sell

The Need

To The love conscious

I'm in desperate need of a backbone
Someone with a stronghold to my inner self
I'm in need of a woman that is soul soothing
With a shoulder and a chest to lean on

I'm in need of a woman that is God fearing
Someone is not only my best friend, but also my equal
Be there for me when times are good and bad
When I'm moody or sad
You can analyze my thoughts
And anticipate my actions to keep me at peace

I'm in need of a support system
If I get locked up
You have my bail money
If I'm off balanced and off track
You keep me on my square

I'm in need of my soul mate
Someone who knows how to keep
The spice in a relationship
Always willing to try new things

Someone who has a spontaneous spirit
I'm in need of your heart
I'm in need of your soul

45
I'm in need of your voice and your touch
I'm in need of love

Time . . . The Anticipation For Love

As I stare into the hourglass,
Each grain of sand falls,
Making it an eternity for your arrival,
Will power is my survival

The use of phone or text attempts,
To hear her voice results in complete failure,
Knowing that at the beginning of this tragedy,
That I failed you

Each grain of sand equals seconds,
Minutes, hours and days,
That passes by awaiting an arrival of someone,
I'm afraid will forever be gone

47

WORDS of LIFE

PART 3

Lost Urban Seed

Lost souls of Generation X
Living day to day carefree
With no reflections of the past
Grade point average 4.0 idiot box 101

Seeds planted with weak roots
Ignoring nature's element of growth and maturity
Infinite possibilities of materialistic longevities lacking
Nourishment from mother Africa

Sunlight nor shine, rainwater, nor drops
Torches of life are passed but dropped
With the whistle of wind blowing through dandelions
In the hood

We must rise

Welcome To the Westside of the Chi

Welcome to the Westside of the Chi
On every block during the summertime
Big Momma's selling fireworks, snow cones,
Hot chips and nachos

Where the sister's got all the game
And the brothers are just flirts
Ladies strutting their hips in stretch denim jeans
And brothers rockin' wife beaters and white T-Shirts

The Westside
Legendary dice games in sidewalks and gangways
Push-up for dubs slap boxing and the younglings' play
Chase the girls, catch the girls, and kiss the girls all day long

The Westside
Flaunting glossed up rides on twenty plus inch rims
Rockin' the latest gear with brand new pairs of
Air Force ones, MJ's sneakers or pink and wheat Tims

The Westside
Where we got the best freestyles and two steppers
Vice-lord burgers, Uncle Remus chicken wings, cheese steak fries
Extra mild sauce and salt and pepper, please!

51

The Westside

Summer hoop tournaments at park districts
With groupies and gang bangers ready to scrap
Neighborhood family fights and battering brothers
Giving their mates the back slap

The Westside
This is where M.J in 88' jumped from the free-throw
Blue flashing lights attached to street poles down a four-mile radius
down Chicago Ave. from Central to Sacramento

The Westside
No need for clubbing' downtown
You can get your party on at a hood lounge
From Austin to Garfield to K-Town, to the Booshwah
Wicker Park and Roger's park. Slide through
Galewood to Oak Park and don't forget that
Hispanic flavor in Mozart and Humboldt Park

The Westside
It's a bad rep with the slanging' fast cash and
Looting, gangs at war with drive-by shootings
We have a good reputation with
House Music Steppin', footworkin', bopping and juking
It's the Westside, welcome

The Queen Bee of Hostility

Why are you so hostile?
Living a life of a ghetto fabulous child
Mother is a dope fiend and sister's a wild child
Father's up in jail and grandmother says
You are no longer her grandchild

Your reasons I believe
But there is no reason for you to be as mean as an
African Bee just stinging away

Each day she steps out of her home
That her and mom shares
As she graces the hood on a hot summer's day
Taking a whiff of the urban aroma
Only to be smelling herself

36-24-36 is the lucky winning numbers to pick for a trick
That gets spoon-fed for brothers who claim titles as ego
Builders to a sister who can't even find

Her own soul to begin with sorrow, sadness, pain and
Suffering clouds her judgments as she succumbs into
Ignorance of sexual pleasure men who shower her with
Brand new pairs of Air force ones and 4pc wing specials
Extra sauce on the side of course

She's lined up to lay with a sea of brothers that
Stretches like the Wu-Tang Clan, never to understand
The price of receiving HIV as a reward for screwing the
Most brothers in the same ward

She flies like the African queen bee
Spreading her honey around over burnt toast
Puts up defense mechanism and stings
Good brothers that can be good for her

In the end, she gets stung

The Question

Where are our black father's?
Black boys who will never see a father figure in action
Will never know how to be a father themselves

We've gone from sad to mad, and angry to violent
400 years can do that to you, but it's no excuse
The mind and body can only take so much
Mental and physical abuse

Where are our black father's?
To teach black girls how to handle a man
Once they become a woman

Teach them how to fight with their minds
Instead of their fist
Teach them to respond with patience
And react with kindness

Three quarters of our black children are born by single
Mothers who are not to blame
Taught their children to fight back as they watched
Us being hung, dragged by horses and split into two
What was she supposed to do?

We left her alone without a clue
Why is it that we make up fifteen percent of the
U.S population, but three quarters of our people

Are piped lined up the jail system
We choose to sell drugs and gang bang
While our foreign friends come in and take all the jobs
We have the nerve to blame someone for our ignorance
We choose to cut school and drop out while federal dollars go towards
programs that skip over our communities
Black men, please answer my question

Where are you?

We Didn't Follow Your Agenda

He would be rolling in his grave
Like a log tumbling down a mountain
How upset would Martin Luther King be
Knowing that we did not follow his agenda?

An agenda that was strong and firm
An agenda that was enforced by a generation
That was hosed, Billy-clubbed and attacked by dogs

An agenda that was ignored because as much as whites
Did not want to integrate with us
Today we choose to segregate amongst ourselves

We've overcome racism at its hardest times
The freedom to eat in restaurants, sit in movie theaters
Hold higher positions in the workplace and most Importantly
the right to vote

We are ignoring what he so dearly worked hard for
As much as whites did not want to integrate with us
We choose to segregate amongst ourselves

The bus boycott agenda was put in place for us to be
Able to sit anywhere on the bus
Even when the bus is empty

The voters rights act was in place for us
But half of us don't hit the ballot box
During the primary elections

We're killing each other, gang violence within
The black communities, drug abuse, and teen
Pregnancy, is an all-out epidemic
Because we choose to segregate amongst ourselves

He died for nothing I guess
If King were alive today, I know what he would say

Shame on us
Shame on us

Heaven Sent

Dedicated to my 1stborn

You bring me nothing but joy
Nervous wreck in the delivery room
Anxiously awaiting my baby boy
Heaven sent

Stress, work, bills, money spent
Remote control on pause when it comes to you
Heaven sent

I witnessed you transcending into this world
March of two thousand and seven
Tiny little frame, from that moment on
Hearing your first cry
My life would never be the same
Heaven sent

Butterfly effect as I reflect on my past
The letters on the page start to shake
I grasp my journal as it took me on a trip to February of 1976
When my mom and dad first witnessed me at birth
Heaven sent moment though I could not remember
I could see two happy people staring down me

Seeing those images made me understand
How precious you are to me
I watch your first steps to the first pair of pull-ups
Your first day of school to your first haircut

From birthdays to holidays
From boy scouts to school plays
I made an imprint on your life
Heaven sent

As I continue to write these pages
I see you crossing multiple stages
Graduating from various grades
And receiving many accolades
Heaven sent

And with God's grace
As I continue to witness you
Grow from a boy to a man
Creating your own life

You will witness the letters on your book shake
And bring you back to a day of reflection
You can understand why you were heaven sent

We Just Don't Understand

As I sit in my four cornered room
Staring at candles Lord
I don't understand why it's not my time to be free

I ask you, God, why this world is full of games
And why it's not my time for fortune and fame
I don't understand that times have changed
And things are not the same

The gas prices are rising like Tsunami
Mothers are crying; our government is lying
Sergeants, cornels, and lieutenants
Are knocking on urban and suburban doorsteps
Giving mama's and papa's bad news

As they take off their hats to explain
Sir and mam your son or daughter died for
Country and for their honor
I don't understand this political drama

Charter schools are up on a rise
Gentrification through public school eyes
Our beautiful black children are transgressing
Through these culturally biased state test scores
With no open doors for the poor

And no chances to restore and cure
And in our black home, we lack that combination
Package male-female Mentor the torch is past but
these days dropped and blown in the wind
I'm trying so desperately hard to understand

We have our young female adolescents
Out on the street exposing more skin
Then mothers can even with the permission to commit sin
Our male adolescents are in high school hallways
Based out like dead zombies with dead faces
Of our ancestors who paved the way for us

But as parents, we spoil our kids with brand new pairs
Of Air Jordan's and Air Force one sneakers as they
Constantly and consistently come home with
C's, D's and F's

I don't understand, is there anything left?

I don't understand why Phat Farm, Tommy Hilfiger,
Diesel, True Religion and P. Diddy
Why they are charging hundred dollars
For a pair of stretch denim jeans and signature shoes

When the Cambodians and Indonesians are making
About eighty to one hundred fifty dollars a month
Feeling and singing the blues

I don't understand why four-year college graduates
Struggle for job placement after graduation
Just for a financial back
But the NFL and NBA steadily spitting out those
Multi-million-dollar contracts to high school students
And most of them are black

But I say is it too late to change?
My deity is constantly calling my name
He's telling me that life and the flesh are not the same
And to stop playing these sinful games
It's a damn shame why momma and poppa
Can't watch her son nourish, blossom and grow
Because for some strange reason
Junior was the first one to go

What about Lil Miss Jo-Jo
Who turned into a high school demo?
She tried to get her GED was conceived by who knows
They say that the boy was twenty-four years old
Slanging' weed and ya-yo He got caught by the po po

And now he's doing two to four
And now she's crying oh no!
Now she stuck with a fat belly to show
This world is so messed up
So please world like Lawrence Fishbourne In
School Daze Please People

63

WAKE UP!! WAKE UP!!

And realize that we are not surprised at the current
State if society that has us sucked up to believe that

WE JUST DON'T UNDERSTAND!!

Daddy's Devil

Daddy's Devil is not the bottle
Not the next-door neighbor or the white man
But the beast that he snorts into his brain

Mixed emotions drive him nearly insane
The fact that daddy denies he has a problem
His pride sinks deep into his soul like the Titanic
The difficulty staring in the eyes of his children
Because daddy's devil blinds his eyes of the truth

Daddy fights this devil every day
And in many ways his family too

Days, Months and years pass
Daddy's devil has a firm grasp
Of his addictive ways
And our silent hearts count the days that past
Daddy gets on his knees to God and asks
Lord forgive me for I have sinned
Wash away this demon and let a new life begin
Daddy's business with the devil is finished
And the result is that his soul has been lifted to
God but not diminished
Daddy lives on

Little Life
Dedication to Pro Life

I wonder how it must be like in there
I see you from a photographic image
So tiny inside your little world
Anticipating coming into mine

I wonder how it must be like in there
Free food, free water, heat, no bills no worries, no pain
If I had super-powers for every child born
These luxuries I would make the same

So you won't see struggle
So you won't feel any pressure
No bad examples
Just a constant change for the better

I wonder how it must be like in there
Not having to worry about being discriminated
Not having endless dreams without anyone
Being able to take them away from you

Not having to be characterized by a number
Or by the color of your skin
Not letting people tell you what can or cannot do
Just living

I really wonder

Big Momma
A Haiku dedication to all Big Mommas who keep our families strong.

Kind and simple heart
Keeping family at peace
Passing torch of love

Ghetto Love

Regardless of what the media shows
And the stereotypes you've been told
Beyond a shadow of a doubt
There is plenty of love in the ghetto

Ghetto love is young boys tumbling in allies
On thrown out mattresses
Young girls playing double-dutch in front of big Momma's house as she
sells penny priced candies with Twenty-five cent little jug juices in
ninety-degree heat

Ghetto love is backyard bar-b-ques
Family gatherings at forest preserves
4th of July fireworks in the middle of the street as
You let the cars pass before you light the stems

Ghetto love is fist fights in allies with best friends
Or strangers, then afterwards
Shaking hands and playing a game of tag football

Ghetto love is bathing your first-born
In a metal kitchen sink even if you
Received an infant tub at the baby shower
Sling shouts made of two by fours, rubber bands, and
Pop bottles

Ghetto love is when families combine soul food dishes

During Thanksgiving and the holiday seasons
Ghetto love is friends and loved ones rallied up
In front of bungalows and two flat housing with flashing
Lights to watch high school sweethearts on prom night
And seniors entering limousines as they prepare to cross graduation
stages

Ghetto love is life
Ghetto love is family
Ghetto love is strife
Ghetto love is harmony

It's nothing but love

We Makin' It – We Be Movin' On

We Stand Bold
Like four hundred years of lost souls
Through blood sweat and tears

As we communicated throughout the years
With Foot stomping and drum tapping
A heroin showed us the way
To follow the drinking gourd to freedom
Willie Lynch, we beat em.'

We Makin' It; We Be Movin' On
From jazz to bebop to swing
From Minton's Playhouse to the Harlem Renaissance
We Makin' It; We Be Movin' On

From blackface to Hollywood
Mammie didn't get a chance to go to her world premier
But it was all good because she paved the way
For Jennifer Hudson, Gabourey Sidibe,
Quvenzhané Wallis and Beyoncé
We Makin' It; We Be Movin' On

From civil rights leaders to doctors and lawyers
To having our first major league Yankee and L.A Dodger
From Jackie Robinson to M.J, black quarterbacks,
Coaches, managers, and owners of the NFL and the NBA
With our First black president of the U.S.A

We Made It, and Let's Keep Movin' On

Act Like That In 85'
A Dedication to Choice Beatrice Peers aka Big Momma

My Young Brothers and sisters
I dare for you to act like that in 1985
Disrespecting and talking jive
Right in your mother's face

Mother looks at you and says
Child you going to have a three hundred and sixty degree
Outlook towards those stars if you don't straighten up
Your face, then she slaps the taste out your mouth

Talking back to 85' moms and pops was like signing your Death
certificate. "Child before you open your lips
You need to go outside and pick out a long nice tree Switch because 85'
parents have an itch for
Tearing up some hide,
Raising their leather belts up in the sky to the
All mighty God Zeus to strike thunder into those behind
As they yell out that famous quote
Before they spank you

"Lord Please, Please, don't let me kill this child."
And when they are done whoopin' you they say
"You know I whoop you because I love you."

Act like that in 85.'
If I recall for you youngling's curfew was 9:30pm

In 1985 you could go to the corner store without getting

Pulled over by P.O, Aunt Flo, Uncle Jo,
Redirecting your behind back to the front door,
Even the neighborhood drunk told you where you
Supposed to go when the streetlights came on

Act like that 85.'
I also think that you younglings are out here glorifying
these rappers knowing that they are
Nothing but artistic prostitutes
Free of charge! Liquor and billboard sponsors
Poisoning our brains and sucking out our pockets
Like vampires thirsty for blood money

B.E.T went from video soul with Donnie Simpson
To twenty-four-hour non-reality television
In 1985 we had channels 2, 5, 7, 9, 11, and
Fox television
Either that or our mom and dad could
Afford a Spectra-Vision

Finally, cable was installed, and we were exposed
To hip-hop, entertainment, and news
Seeing different relations in other parts of the nation

'

N.W.A", Niggas with Attitude
Showed us the police brutality towards
The west coast communities and

I understood that we weren't the only city
With gangs, drugs, and hoods

Act like that in 85.'
I think we are creating too many baby daddies
And baby mommies and we are missing
And needing our big mommies
The big mommies that molded, that scolded us
And kept the family together

She teaches and preaches
And give is those long Bill Cosby speeches
Big momma has the best advice on love, sex,
And all the pieces
To the male and female species

Big momma knows what right and what's wrong
And never lets any controversy prolong

All subjects and situations come to a cease
When big momma speaks
And when she's done talking the problems at peace

She is Big Momma!

She is the central nervous system of
Our black homes today
We miss you; we need you, and we love you

Act like that in 85.'

You younglings are out here acting a little bit too bold

With no one to guide you consult and hold
We've got old dating young and young dating old
We have hoop and rap dreams on every corner

Of every neighborhood
And with this foul language, you are using out here
Bill Cosby said it was up to no good
What good is he showing these days?

Act like that in 85.'
Take a trip back in time with me to realize that
We didn't have much either
But we respected it, and we didn't reject it
The youth these days you take things for granite
Parents need to strengthen their hearts and minds
Throughout these troubled times while dodging

These evil elements outside so I don't have to
Continue to give That Boring speech about how
Things were in 1985

Cherish the Day
A Dedication to the victims of 9/11

I thank Sade for telling the world to cherish the day
Who would believe that when the twin towers fell
Eight years before that she stood across from them on
Top of the world telling us to cherish the day

Guitar in hand
Voice singing to the world curious hearts as they watch
Her many stories high

A beautiful ballad that tells us to appreciate life
A beautiful song that tells us to love one another
A beautiful spirit stood over the universe
To simply tell us to cherish the day

Epilogue

About the Author

Markell Larece Mooney was born and raised on Chicago's west side. He graduated from Kelvyn Park High School, Chicago, IL. Adapting to various cultures was his number one priority. Becoming exposed to the city as an artist and a humanitarian in his community became his primary goal. Markell worked as a teacher for the Chicago Public Schools, teaching Drama. He also was a Poetry writing instructor at a local recreational park in Chicago. Markell is an active member of the Most Worshipful Prince Hall Grand Lodge Of IL, Free and Accepted Masons.

His mother and father raised Markell along with two sisters, and a brother. He was always taught that family always comes first. Values of love and opening your doors to other people stay within his heart. He demonstrated this by creating an outdoor Spoken-word show celebrating over 15 years called "Poetry On The Patio".

In the summer of 2003 Markell dedicated the show to his late father Willie E. Mooney Sr. Since then, the Patio show continues to be a platform for artists to express themselves in the arts and music. Markell has been supporting live open-mic Spoken word events since the mid- 1990's. Markell has been writing for more than 15 years and never had the

thought of performing in front of an audience. Markell is doing something positive in his community to leave a strong legacy.

Markell continues to work on being an ambassador for his community and family. The art of spoken word poetry continues to be a big influence in his life.

Markell's Links & Connects

Official Website
www.wordlifeproductions.com

E~Mail
kellogy76@gmail.com

SOCIAL MEDIA OUTLETS

Linktree
linktr.ee/Kellogy2023

Instagram
www.instagram.com/kellogydapoet

Cover Graphic Designer

Phoenix Xiong imageXcel

(REST IN HEAVEN)

83